alphabet

Rod Campbell

CAMPBELL BLACKIE BOOKS

a is for apple

ready to eat

b is for boots

to put on your feet

C is for cat

sitting alone

d is for dog

chewing a bone

e is for eggs

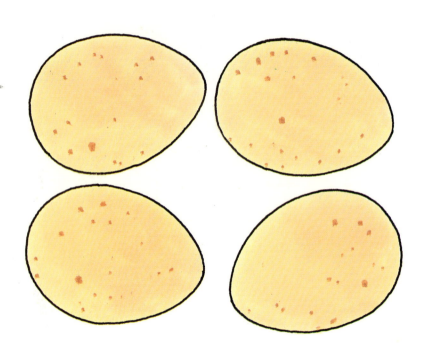

all the same size

f is for frog

with big staring eyes

g is for gate

painted bright red

h is for hat

to put on your head

i is for ice-cream

lovely and cold

j is for jug

with a handle to hold

k is for keys

kept on a ring

l is for lamb

born in the spring

m is for mouse

eating some cheese

n is for nest

that swings in the breeze

O is for octopus

who lives in the sea

p is for piglet

who cries wee wee wee

q is for queen

wearing a crown

r is for rabbit

all white and brown

S is for sun

that shines in the sky

t is for towel

that soon gets you dry

u is for umbrella

to hold over your head

V is for van

bringing the bread

W is for web

where a spider hides

X is for x-ray

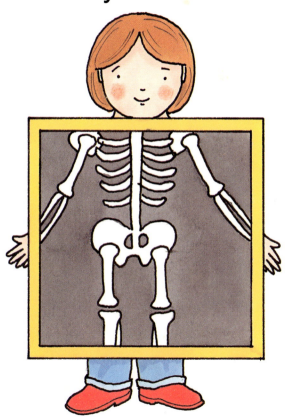

which shows our insides

y is for yellow

the colour of this wall

Z is for zip

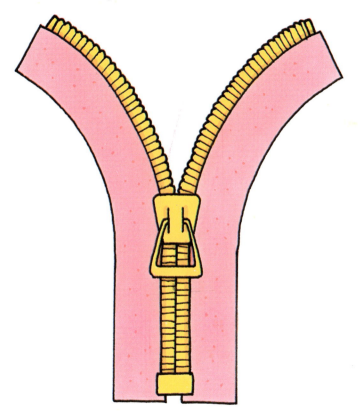

our last letter – that's all!

© Rod Campbell 1988
First published 1988 by
Campbell Blackie Books
7 Leicester Place · London WC2H 7BP
All rights reserved

ISBN 1 85292 013 0

Printed in Singapore